Blinded by the Bling??

The truth about the Trump Organisation plans to desecrate an almost sacred part of Scotland

David Milne

First published in the United Kingdom in 2008
by MilHouse Publishing

ISBN 978-0-9559269-0-7

1. What is this all about?

This is an attempt to put the facts about the proposed Trump Housing Development at Menie, in Aberdeenshire Scotland, in the public domain. There has been a huge amount of propaganda and misinformation circulated to the public, aided not least by some very biased media reporting. This book is necessary because there are some people who actually still believe that this is all about golf. Very little could be further from the truth!

Oh yes, there is a golf course (or two?) involved but there is also a four hundred and fifty bedroom hotel, almost one thousand flats, five hundred houses, thirty six golf villas and a four hundred unit staff accommodation block. Add to that the fact that golf courses don't actually make any real money in the UK at this time and you maybe need to wonder what the motivation is to push ahead with this scheme. Is it really 'all about golf' as the Trump Organisation keep trying to tell us? Or is it simply about profit as usual?

Now there is nothing wrong with making a profit. That is, after all what businesses do and if they don't do that many people would be out of work. But, should profit be at the expense of the environment or a unique landscape that can never be replaced? I, and several thousand others involved in this argument, don't think so.

What cost? I hear you ask, well, the northern end of this area is a Site of Special Scientific Interest (SSSI) which gives it some protection unless the government decided the development is of national significance. This is the excuse that is being used to explain away the special treatment that this development has received all through the process, and as you will see as you read on, it is just an excuse.

This landscape is generally recognised, by anyone who has bothered to get out of their armchair and come and have a look for themselves, as a fantastic and rare place. Undeveloped coast and farmland that has nothing other than a couple of farm tracks and plenty of animal tracks covering it; there is no infrastructure, no roads, no street lighting, little mains water, no mains sewage system or anything like that. It is a place that is dark at night, not flooded with the sickly orange glow of sodium street lights.

This is the way it is meant to be. This place is home to a few people and many hundreds of species of wildlife, according to one of the original letters of objection, up to thirty five of which are listed in the red data book, which means they are internationally recognised as endangered species. One in particular, a specific form of jumping spider has apparently only two habitats in the UK, that may soon be only one.

If the drawings submitted on behalf of the Trump Organisation are to be taken as accurate (they are deemed to be 'indicative, that means they give a general idea but should not be taken as fixed), then this place will become a theme park in the 'Disney Gothic' style with badly designed buildings that take all the character of the area and destroy it whilst killing or herding into ever smaller areas all the rare and vanishing wildlife there is here. At the same time other businesses in the area will be squeezed out and serious damage may be done to the planning system in this country and as for our environmental protection laws, well, they might as well not exist. They are particularly weak as it is, and have been misused in the past, but that does not make it automatically acceptable to ignore them completely.

2. The Area – Where are we and what's so special?

Well the area is one the most beautiful parts of the planet (at the moment) just on the north east coast of Scotland a few short miles from Aberdeen. This area has lacked development for many years as a result of the perceived central belt bias which has never improved, even with the advent of the Scottish Parliament in Edinburgh. If anything it is seen to be getting worse with all the central government funding going to Edinburgh and Glasgow rather than to the productive and forward looking North East of the country. Just look at some of the reasons given for the local argument about council funding in Aberdeen city for more examples of this.

This area, just north of the oil capital of Europe has some spectacular beaches and generally beautiful countryside, almost to the point of being desolate as some have described it. The landscape here has not changed in many years with the 'dunescape' originally being formed some four thousand years ago. What do I mean by dunescape? Well the cover photograph may give you an idea and there are plans under consideration for a photographic book of the area to give you an idea of what we have here, but basically it is a line of dunes, some up to seventy five or one hundred feet (twenty two to thirty metres approximately) high with a flat area, known as dune slacks, just inland of them before the land rises naturally again. At the north end of this area is a sand dome, which was increased in size some forty years ago when a storm broke through the dune line and increased the amount of sand lying in the slacks, this, as a whole, is an impressive and rare site. It is recognised as one of the top five dune systems in the UK as well as one of only two mobile dune systems in the UK and can rightly be called unique in Scotland. It is worth noting that there is an incredible wealth of wildlife in this area with some species struggling to survive in the UK. If this development goes ahead they may only have one habitat left, as mentioned earlier. Surely no one can see that as a good thing??

As mentioned above, the northern end of the site, where several holes in the 'back nine' of the 'Ocean Course' are planned is a Site of Special Scientific Interest (SSSI) which is supposed to give it protected status. South of there, practically all the way to the Balmedie country park is designated as a Site of Interest to Natural Sciences (SINS), this is just a designation and means that the local authority is meant to discourage development in this area (which they have done with fervour until this application came along). A large chunk of the remainder is under the designation of 'undeveloped coast'. This is a European designation and means that even if successful at the National Level, European legislation may prevent this development going ahead. There is also a designation for an area of landscape beauty in this area that also appears to have been ignored. The Regional and Local plan for the area (Local Authority Documents that are meant to look forward to allow planning to take place for zoning and future growth of an area) both say this area is to be left as it is, due to its rare and special beauty. Anyone with a soul who has seen this place understands that it is not meant to be destroyed for profit. Even Donald Trump himself said it 'had been crafted by God' so why is he so keen to re craft it I wonder?

Menie House itself dates from the 14th Century and has a varied past as well as being Grade B listed. Most recently it was the home of another American businessman and lawyer by the name of Tom Griffin, he bought it in the 70s and did a lot of work on the estate and generally restored the house and grounds to something like its former glory. Recognition has to be given to Tom

Griffin for this as the house was almost derelict shortly before he bought it, for what now seems a knock down price, renovated it and added various parts to the building and the estate in a generally tasteful and appropriate manner.

Not far from the house there is a wooded lane known as the 'Green Ladies walk' where, it is claimed, the ghost of a former housemaid is often seen, wearing a green dress. The story is that she hanged herself from a tree in the lane after a failed love affair.

What about Balmedie, the local village, just a mile or two down the coast towards Aberdeen? Well, it is the largest settlement in Aberdeenshire without medical provision. That means there is no doctor or dentist. There is now a chemists shop (pharmacy), two small shops and a post office as well as a new community café. The village is growing with the commuters from Aberdeen clamouring to stay out of town and yet not to have to travel any further than absolutely necessary. The local primary school is here as well, even though there is another smaller one at Foveran just a few miles north at the side of the A90 which, as the main road north, has been overdue an upgrade for at least fifteen years and which is now planned, again. There is no way this small rural village has the infrastructure to support a further two and half thousand people which will be the minimum if this development gets the go ahead. Some of the local inhabitants are in favour of this development, believing the value of their houses will increase and that they will be able to share the gym facilities at the 'resort' with some of the celebrities that are supposed to be going to be visiting. How mistaken they are! Will they be annoyed when they find out they cannot access the site? That they are not welcome and if so who will they be annoyed with?

3. What is planned?

Well that is a good question, if you look at the current submission, the one that is now going to a Public Local Inquiry, it comprises two eighteen hole golf courses, almost one thousand flats (apartments or condominiums), five hundred houses, thirty six golf villas, a four hundred and fifty bedroom hotel, golf clubhouse, driving range, golf academy, turf research institute and various other ancillary buildings not forgetting a four hundred unit staff accommodation block.

Back in May 2006 when myself and the other residents who live within the boundaries of the estate were invited to a meeting 'at Menie House' the emails said, 'come to the side door' was the way it was phrased. When we got there we were directed to the stable block, which had been converted into the estate offices before then, and shown to a tent in the grounds of

Menie House which has been used for several press conferences since. It was not a good start.

At that meeting it was described to us as consisting of two golf courses; maybe two hundred houses, a two hundred bedroom hotel and the other odds and ends that are needed to make these things work. Compare that to the list at the start of this chapter and you will see quite a difference. Maybe more importantly we were told that it would cost about three hundred million dollars and was being done as a hobby by Donald Trump who 'didn't need anymore money'. That was said by Ashley Cooper with Neil Peter White Hobday at his side, a man who appeared very nervous and unsure of himself but seems to have outlasted Ashley Cooper and Tom Fazio II (the original golf course designer), on this project at least.

As I already said there is a considerable difference in the description of what is involved from now to that project outline discussed so long ago. Not to mention the cost of the project which seems to have exploded out of all proportion as time has progressed. Initially it was described as three hundred million dollars and a 'hobby', nice hobby if you can get it. Then, it became three hundred million pounds, then five hundred million pounds and finally it became one thousand million pounds, a nice round billion pound project. Is that really likely? I think not. It makes things look a little more odd if you check into the documents that have recently become available of the Scottish Government website due to the Freedom of Information Act 2002. There is an email from the aforementioned Ashley Cooper talking about the two hundred bedroom hotel and a project, with a total projected spend, of one hundred and fifty million pounds!! Surely international property developers should have a better grasp of the costs of a project before it starts than that.

There is also a feasibility study conducted by Grampian enterprise in 2005 at the request of Neil Peter White Hobday who was, even then, paid by the Trump Organisation for his services. The study talks about the four tower blocks of flats, Benidorms as they have become known locally due to the fact that they are reminiscent of the tasteless timeshare blocks of flats thrown up in Benidorm and thereabouts in the early eighties in order to part the British public from their hard earned money (worth noting is the fact that the Spanish government now discourages this type of development and is actually starting to demolish some of these!!) as well as the two golf courses. It says

"It is currently proposed…that full members will be able to play on the championship 'Ocean' course whilst hotel guests and other visitors will play mainly on the 'Resort' course. If local golfers use the resort, unless they become full members, they will also be able to play only on the 'Resort' course. They may also be restricted to off peak times during the high season for tourists to Scotland and the low season months when tourist numbers are down." Does this fit with the public perception of the phrase 'public golf course' I think not.

The billion pound price tag is a nice advertising gimmick that draws the press and the interest, similar to a one hundred thousand dollar pair of engraved diamond cufflinks that are actually just crystal and can be bought for forty dollars in the local department store. The billion pound price tag is including the housing that is planned to be built as the main part of this development and I believe is possibly the real reason for the development, golf is a side issue. There is a requirement for housing in this area (Aberdeenshire), of that there can be no doubt, but that means that it will be built anyway, by some one, maybe not under the banner of the Trump Organisation. There has been a lot of discussion about affordable housing which is a requirement of the Local Authority planning policies, that it be included within the main areas of housing and not segregated or just 'paid for' with a donation towards it being accepted by the council. Yet here it is described as a 'special case' with no reasons being given why it should be allowed to go ahead without the affordable housing element included within the main development. The cost of housing should not be included in the figure given as investment in an area as it is a recoverable expense, and so will return to the developer as a matter of course. To include it in the headline price of the development is more than a little misleading.

At the departure hearing it became clear that the reason for the housing is simply to allow the whole thing to become debt free within five years. The figures show that it could become debt free anyway, just not within five years

When you take into consideration that the recognised cost for building a golf course, just the course, no clubhouse or other facilities, is only three million pounds; add to that the fact that the projected cost of the Jack Nicklaus development at Ury outside Stonehaven , some fifteen miles south of Aberdeen, is between thirty two million and forty million pounds (half the size at a two hundred bedroom hotel, two hundred houses and one eighteen hole golf course) and the proposed Blairs development by Paul Lawrie is budgeted at one hundred and fifteen million pounds (also about half the size) it raises the question just how much padding is there in the 'headline' price of the Menie housing development. When you also add the fact that both of these developments include a sizable proportion of enabling development (meaning that a large part of the profits from the house building is being used to fund the restoration of a listed or architecturally important building) it becomes an even more doubtful figure.

That is not where the objections end nor is it where the application ends. It needs to be remembered that the hotel and the Benidorms vary in height, depending on exactly which drawing you look at. They vary from eight storeys to twelve storeys, eight storeys is the same final elevation as the council tower blocks at Seaton, which you drive past on your way North from Aberdeen. Twelve storeys is obviously half as tall again. Can this really be said to blend in to the landscape? The length of the hotel structure is almost one third the length of Union Street in Aberdeen and the development strip from the south end of the hotel to the end of the north most Benidorm is almost a mile. That is the full length of Union Street, all the way from the Castlegate to the Holburn Street junction. It will be visible, according to the environmental impact assessment, from as far away as Udny Green, fifteen kilometres away. This is supposed to be in keeping with local design and architectural vernacular!!

4. Local History

Tom Griffin also had plans to build a golf course here but when he could not get backers with the environmental problems and obvious objections to the plan he sold the estate to the Trump Organisation. However, as far as I can tell it was actually a local farmer, James Kidd, who had the idea of a golf course here first. He owned Leyton Farm at that time, which includes the links and some of the SSSI, for many years and finally sold it to Tom Griffin in order to retire with his dream unfulfilled.

Tom Griffin developed the estate by adding to it, when he first bought it there was little more than the house and something of the order of fifty acres, when he sold it, it had just over eight hundred acres. Since the Trump Organisation took it on it has expanded yet again and now allegedly stands at approximately one thousand four hundred acres. Exact figures are varying slightly and always depend on the exact description that is supplied to the Land Registry in Edinburgh.

Late 2005 maybe October or November time, I received a phone call from an individual who identified himself as Peter White. He stated that he had been at Menie house recently and as a result of this wanted to buy a holiday home in the area, would I be interested in selling? The answer was no. It would have been into the early part of 2006 when Peter White turned up on my doorstep accompanied by a blonde woman, whom I believe he introduced as his wife or fiancé (I have to admit I do not remember the name she used, so if you are reading this please accept my apologies). 'Mr White' introduced himself and started by repeating his wish to buy my home, he received the same answer as before. We were not interested in selling, and are still not interested in selling. My website (www.menielinks.com) which I had started previously due to the insistent rumours of a Trump buy out had already mentioned a speculator in the area and that was our initial assessment of his position in the scheme of things; Simply a gambler taking a risk to buy as many houses as he could in the hope of a localised rise in property prices, and in some ways that was the case. One of the other neighbours contacted me by email saying he had been doing a little digging into 'Mr White' who had left him a phone number to call. This neighbour was obviously more interested in selling than any of the rest of us and had called the number. The way the telephone was answered obviously gave him cause for thought as he began to do some more research and he found out that the number was assigned to an organisation known as Hobday Golf Ltd who were apparently not in the best of financial positions having just suffered a major failure of a planned golf development up at Spey Bay, further north than we are in Aberdeen. The plans, which had been to develop an existing golf course with a hotel and some housing, had failed when his US backers pulled out of the deal. This resulted in the operation failing and several local businesses losing a lot of money. Allegedly, Hobday Golf was in debt to the tune of almost one million pounds.

My neighbour was incensed by what he saw as complete and deliberate deception. I can understand his position and do have some sympathy with it, however I also have considerable sympathy for the Trump Organisations position, if they entered a district and began attempting to buy properties as the Trump Organisation the price would go up dramatically due to the name and alleged financial 'weight' behind the name. It is not the first time this artifice was used by people or organisation with a public name or image, the pop star, Madonna, allegedly used a pseudonym when she bought her first London home.

This practice, however, was done so blatantly and in such a short space of time it was immediately obvious that something was not as it seemed. We, as neighbours, do speak to one another occasionally, and as a result we soon found out that everyone had received the same approach at the same time. Would 'Mr White' have been able to buy all the properties, he had offered on if we had all said yes to him, if he had truly been a private buyer? Bearing in mind that under Scots law a verbal offer to buy is legally binding it would have led to an interesting situation.

To be fair to Neil Hobday, he was not being completely untruthful by using the name Peter White, those are his middle names. His full name is Neil Peter White Hobday and he has every right to use those names as he sees fit. It is also quite legal, in Scotland, to call yourself anything you want as long as it is not done for fraudulent purposes. He could call himself Joe Bloggs or John Smith if he saw fit and it would make no difference, he would still not have been able to buy a single property from the occupier at that time.

Their purchase of properties might have been more successful, at least in the case of my neighbour had they been more realistic with the offers they were making. It is my belief that my neighbour wanted to sell and move away anyway for other reasons that are not relevant here. Apparently, the Trump Organisations first offer for my neighbours' house was sixty thousand pounds, for an end terraced villa on three floors with two bedrooms, large garden and a garage. Not surprisingly their offer was rejected, they returned with an offer of ninety thousand pounds which was also rejected. That price at that time would barely have bought a decent two bedroom flat in Aberdeen. I would have rejected it as well. At this point my neighbour decided enough was enough and put his house on the open market publicly stating that it was for sale to 'anyone but Trump'. This was reported quite widely in the local press at the time, and he put it on the open market for offers over one hundred and eight thousand pounds and it sold quickly for one hundred and fifty four thousand pounds. Well done and good luck to him.

At about the same time, one of my other neighbours who lives in a rented property, found that his landlord was changing, from a remote Canadian landlord to the Trump Organisation based at Menie House. This may sound like a bad situation to be in but as they have been in that house for something approaching thirty six years they are classed as 'protected rights tenants', making it almost impossible for the Trump Organisation to move them out without their full consent.

Then there is Michael Forbes whose case is well known and has been written about in many news papers all around the world so I will not repeat the majority of it again here. Mike owns approximately twenty three acres of land in the links area just inland from the dunes, where his family have farmed and fished for many generations (Indeed Menie House was originally owned and occupied by the Forbes family but I am unsure of the connection if any). The Trump Organisation attempted to buy his place, again at a price well below market value, and Mike said no to them in his usual forceful and direct manner. (I know Mike personally and I like and respect him as an individual. He can, however, be very direct in his manner of speaking and does not leave much doubt about his meaning when he disagrees with you.) They apparently have made a number of offers to Mike. None of them being acceptable, he told them to leave him alone. Since then he has had visits from Environmental Health staff of the local authority and the Scottish Society for the Protection of Animals (animal welfare). All of whom have been 'tipped off' or requested to visit but cannot say by whom. None of these organisations have found anything to justify their visit or the initial complaint. The way Mike and Sheila (don't forget Molly, Mikes octogenarian mother who stays on the same site) keep their farm was the subject of the press conference conducted by Donald Trump after they lost the Infrastructure Services Committee vote (possibly to distract people from the facts of that meeting). It was at this meeting that it was described as a mess with rusting tractors everywhere and potential oil leaks all over the place. I would describe that as a description from someone who has never really been out of town much. Mikes place is like any other marginal farm anywhere else in Scotland, the UK or even the US for that matter. There are not enough buildings to keep all the equipment in and when a piece is finished with for the season it is set down out of the way, maybe serviced and maintained but other wise will not be looked at again until it is needed the next year. To describe it as a mess was a very clever trick to manipulate the media into advertising this proposed development around the world.

There have been other minor incidents with many of the neighbours and the attempted reduction of access to the site being reported fairly routinely for a while. Possible one of the best documented was one involving Don Banks who lives in an old lodge house on the estate. One evening whilst walking his dogs, which he has done for twenty five years or so, in the same place in the same manner, he was stopped from walking down the driveway with his two aging greyhounds; The dogs were both in high visibility coats as was Don, but a guard posted on the gate seemed to believe that no one had any rights to access the estate at all that night and definitely not someone who was 'sneaking around'. His supervisor thought the same. They even went to the extent of calling the local police, who were attending another incident elsewhere on the estate at the time. The Police did not help the matter at all by asking that Don go home. This is despite the fact that the 'Freedom of Access, Scotland Act' gives full right to roam to all persons on foot, horse back or bicycle. The only exceptions being any motor vehicle is not permitted nor is commercial activity permitted and access is meant to be kept outwith the immediate curtilage of a dwelling. None of these exceptions applied in this case. It does not bode well for the future of this area when the majority of traffic is pedestrian and may therefore be banned from this area irrespective of the law of the land.

5. *The Planning Process*

The planning process is quite simple really. The law is clear and is undergoing change and simplification as I write. The main act is the Town and Country Planning Act 1997 which is being amended by the 2006 version of the Act. This is coming in, in stages and is fairly well through this process. However it is the '97 version that applies in this case.

The basic process is simple, an application is submitted to the local authority (Aberdeenshire Council in this case), who are acting as the planning authority, they then compare the basic principle against the local plan, regional plan and the development plan (sometimes the same as the regional plan). These are documents that are prepared at regular intervals, usually five or ten years, to allow for planners, developers and members of the public to plan the use of land and where certain main infrastructure elements will have to be developed. If the local authority (usually in the person of an individual planning officer) are happy that it meets all the requirements of the above plans or that there are sufficient 'materiel considerations' to allow it to go ahead. They will then look at the detail of the application and make a recommendation to the actual planning committee, made up of elected councillors, who will either pass or reject it. Some times a smaller application will go on through the process as 'delegated matters' which means that the planning officer will make the final decision so as not to bother the planning committee with minor issues (all being relative of course). If it gets to this stage it then goes in front of the planning committee for determination and if passed may have to go before the Infrastructure and services committee who have to decide if the local authority can afford to supply the necessary services for an application of this type in this location.

That would normally be it, if the Infrastructure and Services Committee passed it, a decision letter would be issued and the applicant could start work. Unless it was in breach of the local or development plans, then it would have to be referred to the Scottish Ministers for their decision. That does not mean an inquiry necessarily. It is possible that the Scottish Ministers could review the case and decide it was acceptable, by simply returning it to the local authority for final determination. If they do think it requires a 'closer look' then they have three choices, written submissions, an informal hearing or a public local inquiry. This particular application has gone to a public local inquiry which starts on the 10th of June 2008.

The time table for the inquiry has been hastened by the fact that it is the chief reporter who is handling this case. This individual does not normally have a case load as such and is usually acting as an 'overseer' or supervisor /

manager of the other reporters. However waiting on another reporter to come free would have taken several months longer or would have the possibility of disadvantaging another applicant elsewhere in Scotland who would have had to wait to have their own case heard. So whilst this is not regular practice it is probably the correct course of action to be taken in this instance.

At the end of the inquiry, currently planned for three to four weeks (but it would not be impossible for it to take up to a year, this has been known before) It is then referred up to the Minister responsible for such things. In this case it is John Swinney MSP, who has the unenviable task of reading the final report and making a determination on this application. He has given himself just twenty eight days before he issues his decision, that may sound a long time but in this instance I have my reservations about it being long enough. He does have the authority to overrule the reporter, whatever the reporter may say, but politically that would be a minefield and is a subject and possibility I would rather not comment upon at this time as I do not want to be seen to be telling the reporter or the government what to do. There are enough other people already doing that.

What is interesting is if you read the legislation regarding the 'call in' process by which Scottish Ministers require the application to be submitted to them for consideration, the language is all about the application having been approved inappropriately. There is not one reference to the call in of a rejected application. This is the first of its kind that I have been able to find any reference to in UK legislation. There is still question about the legality of the call in and this may yet result in a legal challenge which could delay things even further until such time as the European courts can get involved,

There have been several comments where people have stated that they do not understand why a public local inquiry is required. That, again, is actually quite simple, and comes down to the basic SSSI designation itself. Within the Environmental Protection Act (EPA), initially enacted in 1990 and since amended, it states that an inquiry must be held if a designated site (SSSI) is to be the subject of planning permission or other wise damaged / destroyed. This is not an exact quote obviously but is the meaning of the wording. So what this means is no matter when it had been 'passed' or 'approved' it would have been subject to an inquiry.

There are a couple of other points worth noting here as well. First, this is only an outline planning application, so even if it is approved there are still 'reserved matters' to be considered and they will obviously be subject to scrutiny, consultation and rejection, or amendment, or approval, as well. So this whole process may have to be gone through again for each individual element of the application. Secondly, the Trump Organisation had specifically stated that they would not appeal this decision if it went against them. Whether that was a genuine comment or merely another of the tactics that are claimed to have been used by them, throughout this campaign is a matter of conjecture; but the call in was the only way to keep this application live assuming that the Trump Organisation was not going to appeal. So who wanted it kept alive and why? These questions are addressed, if not answered, elsewhere in this book and by many political pundits across the nation at this time.

Scottish planning legislation is tortuous and slow and that is why amendments have been made to the act in the last year or so. Certain elements of the business community want it changed even further and, if the media hype is to be believed, they will only be happy if it reaches the point that any business application receives approval 'on the nod' as it were. I do not believe that is actually the case. Our 'captains of industry' while they may want all their planning applications passed with the least possible fuss and hindrance are not nearly so single minded as to wish to see this country turned into a desolate wasteland. They are after all locals (or some of them stay locally at least) and have a care for the countryside in which they are living as well as taking into consideration the longevity of the planet.

Whilst there is good reason for increasing the speed of the planning process, as it can be detrimental to business, any business, to have progress on a building project holding up the growth and expansion of the company; It has to be done fairly and accurately to ensure that we do not lose that which we cannot replace. This is generally recognised by most businesses that now have a published environmental policy and are judged on their environmental performance amongst other things. Any business destroying a rare and protected site deliberately, would have a hard time convincing clients, customers, and increasingly, staff, that they were a forward looking organisation that truly believed in a sustainable future.

There has also been considerable complaint about the time all this is taking. However it would probably have been quicker if the applicant had appealed the decision of the Infrastructure Services Committee. It would probably have been dealt with almost immediately rather than wait for three months for the Scottish Ministers to decide how they were going to deal with the application and then appoint a reporter etc. Now after the pre hearing meeting etc we have a start date for the inquiry of the 10th of June 2008, almost six months after it was rejected by the

Infrastructure Services Committee of Aberdeenshire Council.

At this point it may be worth mentioning something that was suddenly dropped into the mix back in November or so of 2006 when first mention of a 'planning corridor' was made in outline discussion for the future regional plan. This was to allow a 'corridor' for business related developments up the coast from Aberdeen to Peterhead. This corridor is being called 'Energetica', it is claimed that it will be for environmentally sustainable businesses and lifestyle type developments. If this is true then it would have my support, for what little that is worth, and it may assist with the future development of Menie once this application disappears into the middle distance.

What is relevant here about the plans for 'Energetica' as I understand them, is that a colleague who has had sight of them states that the whole of the route from Aberdeen to Peterhead is allocated for either industry or housing, apart from the area around Menie. It appears undesignated as yet. Now I have not seen these documents myself so I cannot state unequivocally that this is totally accurate but if it is, could this be a coincidence? I doubt it.

6. *Politics became involved*

Politics were involved from day one. This became obvious right from the outset at the Formartine area planning meeting, it was actually hinted at during the departure hearing which took place some time before that. At the Formartine area meeting Councillor Anne Robertson, who is a Liberal Democrat and leader of the council, guillotined the debate by moving it to motion far earlier than had been agreed.

The normal process is that each individual councillor gets to speak and make their position known, this is the first time that they should officially make their feelings about an application publicly known. After each councillor has spoken they then hold a public debate where all the various fine points are discussed and made known to anyone willing to listen. At some point during the debate or more likely after the debate has run its course and discussion is flagging, one of the councillors will 'move to motion'. This ends the debate and allows each member of the committee present to speak once more, for a maximum of ten minutes, before a vote is taken. However that was not what happened this time.

The councillors had discussed the process beforehand amongst themselves, which they are perfectly entitled to do, and it had been agreed that Councillor Loveday as the chairman of the committee, would speak first as no one else was willing to do so, then, they would specifically allow every one of the councillors to speak and have a full debate before any one of the councillors would 'move to motion'. What actually happened was the Councillor Anne Robertson, spoke second, immediately after Mr Loveday, and moved to motion as she finished saying her piece, effectively guillotining the debate and preventing a proper discussion taking place. This caused confusion and upset amongst the public present as well as the councillors. The only ones in the hall who were pleased with this action would be the representatives of the Trump Organisation, including George Sorial and Neil Peter White Hobday, who obviously would benefit from this being pushed through with no discussion taking place. The less inspection this development is subjected to, the better from their perspective as it is more likely it is to be approved.

The facts are quite clear and the more of the public that become aware of them, the less support there is for this housing development, and as a result, there is less support for the politicians who are pushing this unwelcome development forward to approval.

The Councillors were obviously upset and annoyed, possibly even confused by this turn of events. Mr Loveday was able to speak a second time as he had spoken before the call to motion and as such was entitled to speak after the call.

There were no councillors who were unequivocally in favour of the development as it stands, judging from their speeches. Every one of them had reservations about the damage it would do to the environment and the reputation of the North East to so obviously 'roll over' to the threats from the Trump Organisation as well as a number of other issues. Councillor Paul Johnston put forward an amendment to reduce the scale of the development and remove it from the SSSI completely, this was seconded by Councillor Hendry who later voted against the amendment and for the development; which makes it look suspiciously like he was 'reminded' by his colleagues of the party line which appears to be unmitigated support. His colleague who was sitting next to him also described the SSSI as being 'only sand'. This shows a complete ignorance of the facts surrounding this issue whether deliberate, cultivated or natural is up to the reader to decide. The amendment was complex and, I would suggest, confusing to many people including several of the councillors who spoke one way, stated a particular position and yet voted the opposite way. The final result at the end of the evening was that the amendment was defeated seven votes to four. The application, as submitted, was then voted on, and passed also by seven votes to four. This was much to the shame of the North East of Scotland and the glee of the employees of the Trump Organisation who could not wait to telephone their boss to gloat at how well they had done.

The next major step was the Infrastructure and Services Committee (ISC) chaired by Martin Ford. Unfortunately I was unable to attend this meeting due to work commitments but was kept informed by friends who did attend with the help of the trusty and indispensable mobile phone. So please forgive me if the detail here is a little less than elsewhere when I was actually present at some of the meetings etc.

Early on in the meeting it was obvious that almost all of the councillors present, even those who were in favour of the development, had reservations about the scale, the alleged cost and the huge environmental damage the development would do against the limited benefit it would bring to the area. So the same basic process was followed as had been followed at the local planning meeting. An amendment was put forward to reduce the scale of the development to a more realistic size and to move the entire project off the SSSI as per the requests and formal representations of a large section of the objectors and statutory consultees. This was voted on and passed by the councillors by nine votes to five. This meant that as far as the local authority was legally concerned, the original application was dead but for the decision letter, more about that in due course.

The meeting continued and another vote was held, this was between complete rejection and giving approval to the amended version, which basically means sending the application back to the applicant and saying 'make these changes and it will be accepted', This vote was tied at seven votes to seven, and so it fell to the chairman, Martin Ford, to use his casting vote. He followed all existing protocols and process as well as council procedures, if such a thing exists, and cast his vote for the status quo, which means no change to the physical situation on the ground. It was a no vote which meant that the application was rejected!

This was greeted by uproar, initially by George Sorial, who stated something along the lines of "This sends the message, if you want to do big business don't come to the North East of

Scotland" a very inaccurate and biased comment (with good reason), he had obviously formed the opinion that this was going to be an easy victory, that their propaganda and PR machine had done its job. That the hint of a Scots mother and the behind the scenes work with certain businesses and organisations had gained them a victory, before the result was known. This could not have been farther from the truth.

The message that this result sent out was actually a very positive one for the North East of Scotland. It said that if you come to us with a sustainable plan, one that can work, develop the locality whilst protecting the environment, working with nature and not just indiscriminately destroying it as well as considering the local community rather than excluding it completely from the plans going forward, then and only then, will we support you. However if you come in with a bulldozer attitude, expecting the locals, all of us, to be grateful for the 'crumbs from the table', then you are wrong, we will send you away to think again as we have always done. The Scots are a proud race, not easily bought and sold, but one that can negotiate with the best of them and who have dealt their way around the world and back again. We do not take orders well at all, especially not when barked from afar. Negotiate with us and we will strike a deal, or most of us will at any rate, but there has to be benefit to both sides.

It is worth bearing in mind that the definition of sustainability is something that has economic viability, no (or limited) environmental damage and is beneficial to the community, this development does not fit with this definition at all; and therefore could not be supported by any reasonable or realistic business in this day and age.

This council debacle was one of the most disappointing events in the course of things so far and one that was about to get even worse for the reputation of Scotland and some of our politicians. The local press took a hand and one of the most rabid of supporters of the plan was filmed by TV news and in the local newspapers describing the seven councillors who had rejected the proposal as 'traitors to Scotland' and picturing them with neeps (turnips) for a head. This man was only one of many who could not even count or understand the most basic of council practices. The application as it was, had been rejected nine votes to five, not eight votes to seven and after that point there was no physical possibility that the application, such as it was, could be passed. Legally it did not exist, the only catch was the decision letter had not been issued. This was soon to be very important.

The Infrastructure Services Committee meeting had been held on a Thursday, the newspaper mentioned above was published on the Friday. Alex Salmond met with George Sorial and Neil Peter White Hobday at a hotel in Aberdeen on the following Monday and the application was 'called in' by the chief planner on the Tuesday after a phone call from Alex Salmond the previous day. (This turn of events has been the subject of an investigation by a parliamentary committee as well as parliamentary debate and as such will not be gone into any further here.)

There was a lot of discussion about if this was legal or not, but the fact was the decision letter had not technically, been issued. I have been advised that this means, legally, the decision had not been issued. There is still argument about this but it really does not matter. It had been done and that was that. The fine points of the legal process are better discussed by others who may actually be able to do something about it.

Finally most of those in opposition began to realise that this was what we had been after, all along. Legally this was where the application would have had to go even if the council had been 'minded to approve' the application earlier. Even if the applicant had decided to appeal, which they had said they would not do, it would probably have had to go to an inquiry due to the Environmental Protection Act as also mentioned earlier.

Shortly after the Infrastructure Services Committee meeting a special meeting of the full council was called allegedly to change the process in which the council would deal with large or significant applications in the future. Also on the agenda was the removal of Martin Ford as Chair of the ISC. This was a special motion tabled by Councillor John Cox, an allegedly independent councillor from Banff and seconded by Councillor Anne Robertson who is not only a Liberal Democrat and shares the political allegiance of Marin Ford but is the leader of the party and the council. This motion even went so far as to say that even though Martin Ford had done no wrong he had to leave his post as he was sending out the wrong message. The council voted and Martin Ford lost his post as Chair of the Infrastructure and Services Committee simply because he had followed the rules and procedures set down to guide him and other councillors. Very rarely can a person be harried and pushed from their post simply for doing their job as it is meant to be done. What makes matters worse is that the vote was twenty six for the motion, ten against and twenty nine, no votes (abstentions). If this is the way the council votes on a simple 'ejection from post' how are they going to manage to vote and come to a realistic conclusion on any future application of a 'large or significant' nature?

They have merely added weight to the general opinion locally that they, as a body, are a laughing stock and apparently incapable of fulfilling the function which they were put in place to perform.

This is not where the persecution has stopped, Martin Ford has now been kicked off several committees just for doing his job. It came to a head recently when his own political party, the Liberal Democrats, actually debated throwing him out of the party. The motion was apparently withdrawn at the last moment, thankfully, but it was not a very liberal nor democratic thing to do to anyone. I hope this harassment has now ended so we can get back to the serious business of dealing with this application and others that will surely follow.

7. Reasons for supporting the proposals

This should be quite a small section of the story as far as I am concerned, but that would be unfair to the supporters so I will try and give as fair a description of their position as I can.

The main argument seems to lie on the opinion that this is a nationally significant development and that we should do everything in our power to make sure it happens and that this is the right location for the housing development to go ahead. So how is this position achieved? Well the original claims seem to settle around money being brought into the economy and jobs being provided here in Aberdeenshire. Oh and don't forget we have to have something to do after the oil runs out!!

So let us tackle these individually, what about the claim for jobs?

Well that is really quite easy to deal with, the claims in the documents submitted to Aberdeenshire council for their consideration, state that up to six thousand jobs will be created during the construction phase of this project. Unfortunately it does not actually state, in the application, how long the construction phase is expected to last. In one of the supporting documents however it says that ten years would be a realistic period for the construction to last on a project of this size. So that is six thousand jobs over ten years, now that would generally mean six hundred jobs a year for ten years and that is the most likely scenario, which is also stated in some of the documents, so the figure of six thousand jobs is a little misleading to say the least. We are talking about six hundred construction jobs that may last for ten years and would probably be employed here who ever was building the houses.

What about jobs on the site after the work is completed and the hotel etc is actually functioning? Well the same documents that we got the figure of six thousand construction jobs from tell us that up to one thousand two hundred and fifty persons could be working because of this development. That figure includes up to seventy persons in the community outside the gates and fences of the place itself. Now that does not sound like many jobs outwith the site does it? Well there is a reason for that. In most cases of a resort type development, as this is claimed to be, there is a factor called a 'multiplier' used to estimate the number of jobs that would be created in the local community due to the operation of the resort. That does not apply in this case, why? Well, if you read the supporting documents also submitted as part of the application they imply that the expectation is guests will arrive at the site, direct from the airport, and not leave again until it is time for them to catch their flight home. So the local taxi drivers and the shops on Union Street who expect to get a windfall from the overspill of clients visiting the surrounding area will be sadly disappointed. Whilst it is worth noting that the executive summary of the Deloitte report (its formal title is the Economic Impact Assessment and Financial Review. Executive Summary), also submitted as part of the application, states that 'the development returns need to include an estimated amount for the sale of the hotel in 2021'.

Another argument, routinely rolled out, is that this is nationally significant to Scotland, I disagree and so do the facts. One thousand two hundred and fifty jobs (in total) compared to the working population of Aberdeenshire of two hundred and seventy thousand people works out at 0.05%. That is barely significant locally and so I do not believe that can be even close to nationally significant. Also worth knowing is the fact that, at a recent publication point the unemployment register for Aberdeenshire showed a total of one thousand and thirty four people unemployed in the area; not even enough to fill all the vacancies even if those on the register wanted, and were qualified for, the jobs on the site. Maybe that is why there is a four hundred unit accommodation block included in the plans. After all, local labour would not want to go home at night, would they? Surely they would all want to stay on site as long as possible, so they would stand a chance of sharing the spa with a famous star or hero of theirs who so happens to be staying there at the time!!

The economy and its long term impact on the North East is another of the themes being pushed as a reason to support this project. The figure being pushed in elements of the local press and its associates is this completely improbable forty eight million pounds per annum added to the Gross Domestic product of

Scotland, now surely that must be nationally significant to the country, well no, its not.

The last year for which figures were available (at the time of writing) was 2006 and this showed a Gross Domestic Product (GDP) of ninety one billion pounds, that's a lot of money for a small country. Now according to two economists that I have spoken to, this figure is highly improbable, it looks like this figure is the end result of a business plan exercise, which as everyone knows, is a formalised guessing game. Anyway we will use the submitted figures rather than the more realistic twenty million pounds I have been given by someone else. The figure of forty eight million pounds equates again to 0.05% of the GDP. Again, this is nowhere near nationally significant and if you take this against the UK figures it becomes a meaningless dot on the finances. This housing development, even with its ancillary golf course, is nowhere near nationally significant.

So the next argument is tourism, it has to beneficial to bring people into the North East of Scotland, well yes, it is beneficial to bring people here, but, only if they are going to spend money locally that will be of benefit to the local economy. The other side of the coin that is carefully not mentioned is how many people will not be able to come here if this does go ahead? Well, the body that is responsible for trying to bring people here, Visit Scotland released figures early in 2007 for 2006 that showed that only 3% of visitors to Scotland were here for the golf whilst 82% of visitors took part in activities that could currently be enjoyed in the Menie area. These activities would no longer be available to visitors if this housing development goes ahead. So instead of improving the tourism in the area we may actually be turning away those tourists who spend money in the local shops, the pub, the chip shop and the small local hotels as well as in the taxis to ferry them around. This development is likely to do far more harm than good to the local tourism industry.

It is my contention that the arguments for this development as a whole, simply do not stack up. If this was allowed to go ahead, as currently proposed, it would result in a real drop in tourism to the area and any income would be cycled through the corporate machine to the US rather than benefit the national economy of Scotland. It would also tarnish the reputation of Scotland as a beautiful place with a clean and natural environment where people can enjoy the real world. Business wise we would become a target for anyone who thinks money can buy anything and that the people will not be able to argue against it, our planning laws and forward planning of land use and development would become even more of a complete joke than they are already. Our environmental legislation and protected areas may as well all be repealed as they become completely worthless and seen as fair game for a developer who is believed to have a deep pocket.

What about when the oil runs out? I hear you shout, referring to a comment from one of the councillors. Well current estimates for the end of the oil in the North Sea are anywhere from twenty five years to fifty years depending on which data is used, so first of all it is not imminent. Already the major oil companies that are based here in Aberdeen take the most of their profits from overseas, this is stated every year when their profit statements are issued and taxation matters arise along with the wage claims. Many companies based in Aberdeen, city and shire, have large business interests overseas and are only here because it is a common location and the quality of the engineers and support staff are better that they can get almost anywhere else in the world. That is not going to change, the engineers, the specialists and the support teams will still be here in ten or twenty years time. They may be working on wind power or solar energy plants rather than oil refineries and platforms but the basic workload will be the same. Many of the larger companies already have large and growing divisions working on 'alternative energy systems' like tidal power and hydrogen production so the blinkered approach that Aberdeen is an 'oil city' is wrong and outdated. Why else in the All Energy exhibition held here annually? It may not have the same draw as the two yearly oil show yet, but the industry is growing, fast!

Is the leisure industry an alternative as well? Possibly, if it survives; there is no guarantee that this development will work for any of a large number of reasons. The most obvious being that the US financial situation is far from stable and the instability is growing; in the 1990's the Trump organisation almost went bankrupt, according to some stories they only avoided bankruptcy due to a 'mystery gambler' buying four million dollars worth of chips at one of their casinos, and never playing them. I do not know if that is true or just a story, but it is a fact that they, like many others were in deep trouble at that time. The Deloitte document, referenced above states that the development could be put in jeopardy by a financial slow down in the US markets. That is what is happening now and faster than anyone could have foreseen, house sales in the UK and specifically in Aberdeen are also slowing with some new developments allegedly being halted because of poor sales.

8. Reasons to object to the proposals

This is far easier to write as there are far more of them and they are far more relevant to the real world and the people that inhabit it than the reasons in support of the proposal.

As we have already said this is a special and magical place for anyone who is interested in the natural world and that is one of the main objections to this proposal. In this time of global warming when barely a day seems to go past without another species or two vanishing from the surface of the planet by the hand of man, surely those places that are recognised as special habitats for rare and endangered species should be protected at almost any cost. This area as we have said already is allegedly home to over thirty endangered species including one with only two habitats in the UK. Even the casual observer will see the amount of wildlife here is phenomenal. Foxes, badgers, deer and otters are prolific here as well as Kestrels and Buzzards and many other species that I, as a layman, cannot identify. The wildlife growth in this area has been noticeable since the estate began to be used as a shooting estate by Tom Griffin several years ago. This is due to the increase in bird food that was available as well as ground cover crop that protects and shelters the young, and sometimes not so young, birds from their predators as well as the oft present, bone chilling, haar during the summer months.

The weather in itself is a concern for a development of this type, up here in the North East of Scotland we have a huge number of golf courses, seventy two or so I believe including the two that are being championed by recognised international standard golfers at Blairs and Ury, both outside of Aberdeen, although one is barely south and the other inland (West) a little. The problem is that quite recently several of the clubs actually had to consider closing down due to there not being enough golfers to keep them open. This was partially due to the weather here, the old joke about 'if you don't like the weather wait ten minutes' can be almost literally true. The wind and rain are absolutely horrific and unpredictable at any time of year, next to the sea it is even worse. There is the added hazard of the haar, mentioned above. An infamous coastal fog that many people just seem to be ignoring at the moment; on a fine summers afternoon it just seems to roll in out of nowhere up to maybe half a mile or a little further inland with a bone chilling cold that drops the air temperature by up to ten degrees centigrade and can restrict visibility to an unbelievable extent. It usually occurs during the summer months when inland towns and villages are enjoying a beautiful summers day, the coast is shrouded in a cold, wet, gray blanket. There is nothing that dampens the spirit more than driving to the coast on a summers evening to see that gray line of fog just in from the coast and to know that your car will be shrouded in it shortly, beading on the windows and on the clothes of anyone who dares to go out in it. This is one of the other main reasons that the Open Championship will probably never come here. They (The Royal and Ancient) are unlikely to risk a competition in a place that they cannot be at least sure of the weather to a degree. I wonder how many of the readers of this little book will remember the year when the open was held at Carnoustie and the players almost walked off the course because of the wind? Well just imagine the same type of wind with either sand in it or the cold, clammy, gray fog, billowing across the course so they cannot see half the length of the fairway let alone where the pin is.

Just up the coast is the Forvie Sands National Nature reserve and it is generally accepted locally that the windblown sand from the links here is at least partially what feeds the reserve and keeps it going. It is highly likely that if the sand here is 'stabilised' (or 'locked down' as it has been described), then it will have an adverse effect on Forvie. This movement of sand has been researched, pictured and recorded by one of the local residents and was presented at the departure hearing many months ago. It is likely that many of the people present did not understand the import of what was being said. It is quite something to see when the wind blows the sheet of sand drifting like snow across the ground at a high speed.

One of our other main concerns is that if this does go ahead and it is found, as many people believe, that it is impossible to anchor the sand, how long will the course exist?

Meanwhile there appears to be a new sand dome forming, down at the North end of Balmedie Country park, south of this area and even the comments of a supporter of this housing development bear out that this is going to gradually move northward and obliterate anything built in its path. This individual is a fifty one year resident of the area and he has been quoted as saying that the current dome 'was not there forty years ago. It was half a mile further south'. That is the whole point that we are making. Even a casual review of the old Ordnance Survey maps of the area, from 1869 or so, and up to the present day, show the dome, and therefore the sand, in constant motion; the gap between the update of each map varies as does the location of the dome. It all depends on the weather and how hard and often it comes from the sea. Stabilising the sand that is there at the moment will not help, even if it succeeds. There is always sand coming from the south to infill the area and work its way up the coast. Apart from anything else, marram grass, which is what they want to use, has a very particular way of stabilising sand. It is triangular in shape and it works by causing a small still air pocket behind it, so that when sand is drifting past it falls into the calm 'pocket' of air in much the same way as snowflakes do to form a drift; the exact same thing happens here, except when it is sand we call it a dune. So by planting marram grass they may actually be causing dunes to form. Exactly the opposite of what they want to happen. I would expect, however, that the developers will have taken professional advice about this, no matter, I am still sceptical.

Surely the costs of excavating the course every time there is a storm or even just a decent wind, will soon make it uneconomic to continue. Then what are we going to be left with? Probably a complete eyesore and white elephant as the towers crumble from disuse and blight the landscape for miles around – as they will do even if it is successful.

A similar thing could happen with a simple summer storm. When the wind gets up enough here and it breaks the dune line, as it has done many times before, it starts to spread sand in behind it. This can be easily seen in several places along the coast, the most obvious one being the actual dome which was dramatically increased in size about forty years ago after a storm broke through the dune line just south of the dome and added to its surface area. But even a casual observer, at the moment, can see breaks where sand is encroaching on the inland area as described above. This is a natural happening and man has rarely succeeded in taming the powers of nature.

The Deloitte document, or at least the executive summary, warns of the effect of an economic slowdown and here we are with the US in the worst economic situation that has been seen this century. Tourism from the states is already down noticeably and there is no indication of an improvement in things anytime soon. Add to that the fact that the golf tourism industry, what this development is allegedly all about, has been in decline in the states since about the year 2000, with no increase in overall revenue irrespective of the number of resorts available. There are growing developments in Brazil and Kazakhstan, feasting off the local oil industries there, but, if as the supporters say, the oil is about to run out here then who is going to play here? No one, is the most likely answer and the wind will howl through the broken windows of the empty condominiums just like it does down round the rock at Blackdog or maybe it will be the equivalent of the bell ringing in the church tower at Forvie that was supposedly buried in a sand storm in the year 1413 as a warning to other unwary developers.

Then there is the local financial argument, it is worth taking into consideration the story that has unfolded at St Andrews with the Fairmont St Andrews Hotel, a newly built resort at the home of golf. St Andrews, a town often known as the golfers Mecca, where every golfer from around the world wants to play at some point; The Fairmont St Andrews Hotel was built within the last few years on the outskirts of St Andrews to cash in on this fact and is struggling quite badly to achieve anything like the success that was expected of it. In the last year that published figures are available for it lost some where around three million seven hundred thousand pounds (£3.7M) and since its opening has lost fourteen and a half million pounds (£14.5M). If it cannot succeed in the 'home of golf' how will it succeed elsewhere? Add to that the basic figures, if we are generous and allow a seven month season with no off days and a foursome of golfers teeing off every fifteen minutes without fail (more than a little optimistic, I know, but lets be generous for a minute here) that is one hundred and ninety two golfers a day. Assuming a green fee of only two hundred pounds per person (Kingsbarns at St Andrews apparently charges around £175 per round where as others over seas charge several thousand a round) that is an income of seven million five hundred twenty six thousand, four hundred pounds a year (£7,526,400 per annum). I am not a financier but I do not see how that is sufficient to even begin to pay back the interest on one billion pounds. Also if you have one thousand five hundred accommodation units and only one hundred and ninety two people can play golf in any one day what are the other one thousand three hundred and eight going to do all day long? (That is assuming only one person per hotel room or apartment and ignoring the houses entirely) Or are they expected to stay around for at least eight days to ensure they get a turn to play?

Another aspect of the financial issue is the houses and flats they want to build here. Approximately five hundred houses and almost one thousand flats in four tower blocks; how many Americans (that is the target market after all) will be willing to spend one million dollars on a home in Scotland that is going to squeezed onto a small site in the hope that they will be on, or close to, a golf course that may one day host the Open Golf championship (which we doubt it will ever do). At this time I very much doubt that will happen. I have friends in the States who are in the realty business (they would be called developers and estate agents in the UK) and they are having a hard time just now. It does not seem to matter whether it is sixty thousand dollar homes or one million dollar homes, very little appears to be selling. People are scared just now of how far down the financial markets are going to go. I do not believe it is really likely that people who will not buy, at home in the US, will buy overseas, here in the UK.

Why do I say a small site? Well as part of the public campaign, at the local authority stage, a local man who trained as an architect, built a model of the proposed development, to scale from the drawings submitted to the local authority. Using standard sizes for dwellings he found it almost impossible to fit the five hundred houses onto the site shown on the drawings for them.

This model has been criticised by Neil Peter White Hobday of the Trump Organisation, who described it as 'indicative' when he saw it outside the Balmedie Primary School during one of the council meetings. That is hardly surprising as it is based upon indicative drawings. However if the model is inaccurate as has been suggested, what does that say about the drawings that it is based upon? Can we trust them? Before the first meeting in the tent at Menie House, Donald Trump spoke to us as a group and he commented that 'you only need two hundred acres to make a golf course, you can actually do it with one hundred and sixty. We've got eight hundred (that was the size of the estate originally) so we can move it about a bit'. So, if that was accurate then, and I have no reason to doubt him, can someone explain to me why there is this total resistance to do so now? Also if you look at the submitted drawings you will see that the area marked for 'future golf' is a lot smaller than the initial course and is in two sections. A lot of people believe the second course will never be built and that this area will end up, if the project goes ahead, as more houses on a flood plain. We will have to wait and see on that one.

What about the infrastructure? That is simple, there is none. On a very basic level the sewage works in Balmedie are almost at capacity between the existing load and that already accounted for with new development on the south side of the village. The waste from Newburgh up the coast is already pumped, at high pressure, through the estate down to Balmedie. The primary schools are close to, if not at capacity; Ellon academy for the older children is also pretty well full. Add that to the facts that we discussed earlier in this book,

Balmedie has no medical provision at all, the roads are under planning at the moment with no allowance for this development; Even though that last sentence may not be entirely accurate. There was an exhibition held at the 'White Horse' hotel in Balmedie relatively recently where the plans for the dualling of the A90 were open to the public for examination. Discussion with the Roads Authority personnel made it clear that discussions with the Trump organisation have taken place and that they (the Trump Organisation) are aware that if the development gains the approvals it requires then any special junction required would have to be paid for by them. It has also recently come to light (April 2008) that the road works have been delayed for another two years and will not now commence until 2010. Is this another case of the locals suffering in order to ensure politicians achieve their goals? This road improvement was described was 'imminent' when I moved into the area fifteen or more years ago. Why are the local population being made to wait yet again, for something that will probably never happen??

It is worth considering that if there were to be one person in each flat and house (ignoring the hotel) that means a minimum of approximately one thousand five hundred vehicles added to those on the A90 every day. That is just not practical for this area at all. The ring road (Aberdeen Western Peripheral Route) is supposedly started, but they have been arguing about it for sixty years already so don't expect any final answer or actual construction work soon.

The infrastructure of this area has been neglected for decades and is simply not up to the additional load that a development half the size of this would impose. If it does go ahead and the infrastructure requires to be improved, which should happen anyway to a far lesser degree. Then, the local authority will have to fund it, as I believe it is unlikely that the Trump Organisation would be willing to negotiate on this topic. If the local authority has to fund it that means that the local populace will have to fund it. It is clear from the current situation with Aberdeen City being financially short by twenty seven million pounds that the Scottish Government, who appear to be supporting this development wholeheartedly, will not fund it even though they are being blamed for the shortfall that the council are now suffering from.

9. The Supporters

There are many supporters of many different persuasions and most, if not all of them believe they are doing the right thing, but have they been 'Blinded by the Bling?' That is the question posed by this little book. A large proportion of the supporters are in the business community and are probably looking at what they believe are opportunities for them to profit and grow their businesses. Good, that is what any business person should do and it is commendable that they are looking forward and keeping up the history and reputation of the North East of Scotland as a centre of business excellence and innovation. It is worth noting that it has recently been announced that this area is the best in the UK if you want to start a new business. The number of successful new and expanding businesses here far outstrips the national average. This presents another factual problem for those who claim we have to find something to do after the oil runs out.

The local Chamber of Commerce has done an excellent job of coordinating efforts to support growth industries here in the North East and should continue to do so in the future. However, I and many others believe that they have made a mistake this time. The Trump Organisations local Marketing person, Lora McCluskey, made a number of presentations to the business community via the chamber of commerce meetings and basically asked them to support the application as the number of objections far outweighed the number of letters of support. This is evidenced in a number of the letters of representation made to the council which actually quote this as fact. Now, there is nothing wrong with canvassing support for your position and the use of standard, or rote, letters is accepted practice as well. The problem lies in the fact that these statements were made at a time that information on numbers of objections and letters of support would not normally be available. As I understand it, numbers of representations are not available to the applicant or their agent until almost the last minute, so was this yet another case of this application receiving special treatment, or have I misunderstood something?

Many local businesses, such as taxi drivers and the local pub (The Cock and Bull) seem to believe that they will gain an increase in trade and business from this development and as such are in support of it in all aspects of its business. That may be why after the Infrastructure Services Committee decision they put up two rather inflammatory notices for a period, with no evidence of planning permission for them. As discussed earlier, the plan is to ship customers in and keep them on site before shipping them back out to the airport. The whole business ethos of a development like this is to keep the customer on site for as long as is possible and to minimise the 'off site spend'. The local businesses will not gain a great deal from this development, if anything at all. It is reported that at least one business that was operating locally, a pest control firm, took on a contract for the Trump Organisation and after a short period of time was bought out by them to become a wholly owned subsidiary. Now obviously the business owner was happy to sell his business other wise it would not have happened, but the impact of this is that one independent business has been lost to the North East. I do not know what the terms of the deal were and I have no right to know, but is it not possible that the services of this business are now no longer available to other operations within the area? If that is so, what will happen when the application fails, or the development undergoes financial collapse after a couple of years? Does this mean that yet another business will not be able to be resurrected due to contract clauses that prevent restart of a business within a specified time frame and as such will the businesses former owner and any staff end up as benefit claimants? There have already been redundancies amongst the staff who used to work on Menie Estate.

There are still a few members of the public who are in support of this application but many of these are individuals who have not been properly informed of what is actually proposed. The vast majority of these people change their opinion once they realise what is actually planned and the damage this development would do to both the environment and the reputation of the North East. These people are not to blame for their lack of understanding, a large proportion of that culpability has to lie with the local media, in particular the two main newspapers in the area who have disgraced themselves not only in the eyes of the local population, but the national and international media who now view them as a laughing stock due to their biased and inaccurate reporting of the matter. The letters pages in particular became a source of amusement as they continually printed letters of nothing but propaganda and awarded them star letter status. Not to mention the now infamous Smith and Jones letters. Many letters objecting to their handling of the matter and pointing out the failings in both the development and the arguments supporting the development were not printed and many of us doubt they were even read. Meanwhile, the quality papers, more used to dealing with larger issues and long term impact rather than minor parochial details, printed many of these letters and gave a far more balanced view of the facts. They even allowed us to post to their online reports and articles which somehow seemed to be impossible for many of us with the local papers and their websites.

The Scottish National Party seem to have taken a party line on this issue, which would have to be unofficial for obvious reasons but it does tend to show quite clearly that many of our independence minded politicians seem to have an almost 'Blairite' tendency to follow the leader. After all it doesn't matter how wrong he may be, he is still their leader. It does however beg the question whether they do actually want independence or if they merely want to swap the 'yoke of Westminster' to start 'working for the yankee dollar' instead.

10. The Objectors

Who are we? Some of us are local, some of us are neighbours, some are strangers from afar, but the one thing we have in common is a belief that this development is the wrong one for this location and that the long term cost to the people of this country is far too high.

The vast majority of objectors are individuals who have decided to take a stance and point out to the rest of the population what they already know, that this development is unjustifiable and unacceptable in many ways. These are people who care about what happens when big business meets the environment and a biased political system, both locally and globally, ignore the obvious facts in order to make political gain.

However there are also the specialists, people and organisations which were set up and are paid to provide expert advice and guidance, as well as some charitable organisations who are almost all primarily interested in the environmental side of the issue, and almost all against this development and the damage it would cause. As far as I am aware there are no external bodies in support of this application other than the Chamber of Commerce, whom I believe to be acting out of the correct intentions but are merely misguided in their beliefs.

One of the leading 'organisations' that is standing up to the developers here is Sustainable Aberdeenshire who are a very loose group of people with no formal constitution or even a committee. These are merely a group of individuals who have come together to fight what they see as imbalance and unfairness in the process that may ultimately lead to an environmental catastrophe. The possibility of which appears to be being carefully and deliberately ignored.

As a group, Sustainable Aberdeenshire has had a global effect in raising the awareness of the public of the damage that can happen when developments like this are allowed to happen unchecked and unscrutinised. A small group of individuals who seem to be the nucleus of Sustainable Aberdeenshire are going to be represented at the Public Local Inquiry by John Agnew, a planning agent of some repute, generally recognised to be one of, if not the, best in the country at pointing out the facts and getting to the truth of a situation like this, where the rule of planning law may not have been followed as closely as it could have been. These four individuals have a variety of reasons for their objections and opposition to the planned housing development and as these are well enough described elsewhere it is not necessary to repeat them here.

Between them they have a large variety of knowledge and experience which has proven itself invaluable to this discussion in that it has brought a lot of information to light that might otherwise have remained hidden for a lot longer than it already has. The formal position of these people is the same as it always has been, they are not opposed to the idea of a golf course, but see no reason why it should be built on protected land that is completely irreplaceable. The Hotel is out of scale and completely out of keeping with the local vernacular as are the tower blocks and the thought of housing in a location where there is no infrastructure; either present or planned is ludicrous. Even a recent survey conducted by the local authority amongst property developers in the area did not identify this area as a preferred location for building a new town, which is what this, effectively, is.

The special treatment this application has received has also bothered many people, bearing in mind the number of planning applications that have been refused in this area for very specific reasons. Not least that previous and current owners of parts of this, and other Sites of Special Scientific Interest have been advised that they 'could not even put a spade in the ground' yet the Trump Organisation propose to stabilise it and remove the very reason for its designation. It is then with disbelief that people see this development being marked for approval even though it also breaches these same specific reasons by a far greater margin than any of the previous applications. It is very sad to see the principles of the local authority being ignored and by passed in such a blatant and irresponsible manner.

11. The Campaign

The campaign relating to this housing development has obviously polarised into two distinct camps, one for and one against. The campaign in support of the housing development has been quite slick and well orchestrated. The Chamber of Commerce have been instrumental in using their influence with certain local businesses never missing a trick to try and convince other local business people to support this by continually bombarding them with 'information' (sometimes called propaganda) that explains all the benefits of the development. This included the use of the Chambers own monthly magazine as well as a few carefully selected 'interviews' in the local newspapers again putting over, very forcefully, only one side of the story. The local newspapers have had a major part to play as well with a lot of very specific coverage of certain aspects of the campaign along with a few pictures of the opposition, quite often followed by pro development text. Even the local radio station got in on the act with an interview being held with Councillor Martin Ford, it did not sound fair or unbiased to me.

For a long time the supporters of this iniquitous development seemed to be having it all their own way as far as the publicity went. The local papers just ignored any press release sent by the opposition but were conducting numerous 'interviews' with the supporters. This has now been taken to another level by one of the local papers who will be running free advertising for the development in the form of interviews with Donald Trump in the weeks leading up to the Public Local Inquiry; so much for a balanced and fair media.

It has often been said that 'it is easy to object but difficult to support'. Never has that been further from the truth in a free country. The websites that were set up to let people know the facts of the matter were initially receiving very little traffic and yet a petition in favour of the project was widely publicised by the local media who initially ignored opposing petitions. It was not until Donald Trump himself made a visit to the area, shortly after the Infrastructure Services Committee decision to throw out his application, in order to bolster support after his team failed in their initial objective that the opposition were really recognised as even existing. Donald Trump launched an unprecedented verbal attack on a local man, Michael Forbes, at the press conference. That attack went round the world on the media in a matter of hours. Was it a mistake as many have said? I don't think so. Donald Trump is the self professed king of self publicity and even states in one of his books 'there is no such thing as bad publicity'. It is my opinion that he knew exactly what he was doing at that press conference and in a few minutes he achieved for this development what all of his (probably) highly paid and (almost certainly) highly experienced PR team had failed to do in several months. In a matter of a few short hours while the news media carried the message of his verbal outburst around the globe, every investor that he could not otherwise reach knew that Donald trump was planning to build a housing development at Menie in Scotland.

The opposition on the other hand did not have the means or the facilities or the draw to call a press conference and get the interest of the media, particularly the local media who acted (and are still acting) as if the opposition didn't exist. So they started on a small scale as individuals each writing their own letter of objection to the authority and reading the submissions as they appeared on the council website scanning through the pages of copied and unqualified support that gave no reason for support looking for valid points. Gradually it became clear that there was a large and substantial number of objectors, possibly even in the majority of individuals in the area.

I received an email via my website (www.menielinks.com) advising me that there was a meeting being held in Aberdeen and asking if I would advertise it on my website, this I did, and Sustainable Aberdeenshire came into being. That first meeting was attended by a total of fourteen people. Two of whom left about half way through the meeting when the question was raised were there any supporters of the proposal present? They have not been seen at any of the subsequent meetings, but we are still convinced that there are supporters on our email lists. Such is the way the game is played. Other meetings have followed and interest and attendance has grown. Emails have been received from around the world in support of our campaign against the development and whilst taking great care to be fair and remain polite and still staying away from the personal attacks that have been so prevalent amongst the supporters of the development we have produced and issued numerous press releases and a number of other documents that have been picked up by the international media. However, one of the websites (www.meniescotland.co.uk) had a forum, for discussion amongst all interested parties, and it was working well until immediately after the Infrastructure Services Committee decision. It became necessary at that time to shut down the forum due to the level of profanity and general abuse that was being thrown at members of the opposition campaign by a very select group of supporters of the development. These same individuals succeeded in shutting down a discussion forum on a website run by a national newspaper due to the same tactics, basically profanity and base insults. It would be very interesting to find out if any of those posting to the websites of 'The Herald' and 'The Scotsman', the national newspapers mentioned above, had IP addresses located in New York even though they were presenting themselves as being local to Aberdeenshire. The newspapers involved should be able to identify if this is the case or not. I raise this because another website run by a student and very new on the scene as I write, had two individuals join the site and register with free email addresses, one was @yahoo.com and the other was @gmail.com, giving no indication of their location. However the IP addresses, logged by the internet provider hosting the site, were located in New York and assigned to the Trump Corporation. This does not mean that the Trump Corporation had anything to do with these people and their actions. It may just be two people 'doing some surfing' in their lunch break. It is also worth noting that at the same time as these people were logged on, there was an attempt to access the control panel for the website, again there is no guarantee that these people were responsible for this, it may be purely coincidence. However it is disappointing that people cannot allow others a differing point of view without resorting to these types of tactics.

Also worthy of recognition and thanks are the large number of people who gave up their weekends for a good amount of time to populate a stance in the middle of Aberdeen to allow members of the public to see the model that had been constructed for this purpose, and to make available petitions that could be signed or previously prepared letters that could be taken away and amended or just signed by the public to register their opposition to these plans as currently submitted. It was quite amazing how many people still thought it was 'just a golf course'. Some of those people presenting the facts were insulted and told they were fools, sometimes by those same people who thought it was just a golf course. But they stayed there and made sure that the truth was made available to the general public if they wanted it and increasingly they did want to find out the facts. The close proximity of Union Street, (approximately the same length as the whole development from one end of the hotel to the far end of the Benidorms) and the council offices (about the same height as the hotel) helped for comparison.

During the initial stages of the application process before the Formartine area planning meeting a short DVD was produced which was sent to all the relevant councillors and the members of the Infrastructure Services Committee. Once the Infrastructure Services Committee had rejected this application, the video was extended to include a plea to push for a Public Local Inquiry and this was sent to every member of the Scottish Parliament at Holyrood. I do not know if they all watched it or maybe used it as a coaster for their coffee cup, but some of those who have sent replies have been very supportive. Did it have any effect at all? I do not know, but I saw it (and still see it) as a necessary step in the process to attempt to convince the relevant people to do what is right and refuse this application to destroy the countryside.

Those same people, and many others, who had stood in the cold on Union Street and in front of the St Nicholas centre all turned out at Newburgh on a cold Saturday morning in November 2007 to march along the beach to Balmedie Country park to show their opposition to this development. Approximately two hundred and fifty people turned up along with television news crews and documentary film makers and even some of the local newspaper reporters, it doesn't sound a large number but when you consider we did not really get any advertising or media coverage in advance of the event, the turnout was good. Add to that the fact it was a cold November morning when many people would normally have been out Christmas shopping, and the wind was from the south, meaning that the walkers had sand blowing into their face for the full length of the walk. You have to give credit to these people and the depth of their belief that this development is not right for this location.

Now we go forward to the Public Local Inquiry to see what will be said and what the outcome will be. The local Authority have reinforced their position as the local laughing stock by putting forward a submission in support of the development even though the last legally held position of the council as Planning Authority was to reject this application. This, according to our planning agent and a number of legal professionals who have written to the press, is not a legally valid position and is a deliberate attempt to deny those members of the council who support the position of refusal, the legal representation that they are entitled to as those presenting the formal position of the council as the former planning authority. It will be interesting to see what the reporters make of it.

The Trump Organisation has retained a high priced and well respected QC to make their case for them. Whether or not it will help is another matter. It really is almost irrelevant who presents the case, the facts are the same. The difference an individual can make is in their understanding of planning law and practice as well as, more importantly and almost indefinably, their belief and conviction in their cause. Time will tell.

In a new and somewhat surprising development the Trump Organisation has withdrawn another application they had running in conjunction with this one. In addition to the outline application for the whole development they had a detailed application in for just a championship golf course and driving range (under reference number APP/2007/1517). This was probably lodged in the expectation of gaining approval from the Infrastructure Services Committee and in the hope that final approval would be quicker so they could actually start work sooner. Quite a clever idea and if the initial application had been approved as they expected, the construction may even have been started by now (April / May 2008).

So why have they withdrawn it? Well it may just be for simplicity to allow them some more manoeuvring room in the actual inquiry. An outline application is 'indicative', it gives an idea of what is planned, what the principle being applied for is, whilst a full planning application is a fixed representation of what is planned. To make changes to a scheme of development based on an outline approval is easy, it happens at the reserved matters stage. To change a full approval requires an amendment to plan, a formal process that can require a lot more work and time.

It is also possible that this is the first sign of the Trump Organisation considering taking the golf course off the SSSI. If the full application was still live it would be difficult for them to do this in the Inquiry, but with it withdrawn they have a few more options available to them.

Let us wait and see what happens at the Public Local Inquiry, that is where the decisions will be made visible.

12. The Media

The media, generally, have had a field day around this situation both locally, nationally and even internationally. The world is watching Aberdeenshire Council make a mess of things as well as a fool of themselves. Radio and newspaper interviews have been given by all parties to the dispute, and a fair number who have no direct involvement at all, to, amongst others, The Wall Street Journal, CNN, ABC as well as the BBC and Scottish television, not forgetting Vanity Fair. Documentaries have been made with Dutch and Spanish television as well as the BBC and there has even been an approach from an Arabic television channel wanting to do a piece. It is important that this is handled correctly otherwise we, the people of Scotland, lose all credibility and will no longer be able to stand on the world stage and advise other countries what they should and should not do with their countryside for long term economic development in anything remotely like a sustainable manner.

The media need to take out the message to the world that strong sustainable development is what Scotland is both wanting and requiring. Short term destructive developments are not welcome here, or anywhere else for that matter. We need to learn from Spain that is now discouraging the style of developments that initiated the nickname 'Benidorms' for the proposed flats at Menie.

The national and international media have behaved, generally, very well giving a balanced and realistic view of what is planned and the detrimental effect it would have on the dune habitats and biodiversity here which is acknowledged by even the Trump Organisations own Environmental Statement. This and the involvement of an international figure such as Donald Trump, who is his own media machine, has ensured a high level of international interest that some of the local media and populace are only now beginning to appreciate the power of.

As is to be expected, the local media has been split with some being realistic and objective whilst others are being parochial and narrow minded as they were always expected to be. It is disappointing that an area, such as this with a large amount of influence on the international stage should have such a narrow representation in the local media. It will be interesting to see as time moves on how, and if, they learn from their humiliation on the world stage at the hands of their fellow reporters and grow into a media that can be accepted and taken as a true representation of the North East of Scotland on the world stage.

13. What happens next?

Well, what happens next is completely up to the reporters who have been selected to hear this case. These are professional people who do this routinely, usually alone with professional advisers, and listening to submissions from highly capable lawyers and others including expert witnesses and Queens Council. An obvious indication of how seriously this matter is being taken is that three reporters have been appointed to sit on this inquiry, rather than just one. One of whom is the chief reporter and therefore has a large amount of experience and knowledge of similar situations to draw upon with which to evaluate the evidence and come to a conclusion.

I have to admit to not having any experience with Public Local Inquiries and what little knowledge I have is recently gained. It is, however my understanding that the basic rules of an inquiry are purely around the planning law and guidance, taking into consideration all 'material considerations' relevant to the situation.

Some have said that an inquiry can only approve or reject an application but my reading of the legislation, and discussion with those far more experienced than I am, leads me to believe that a reporter (or panel of reporters in this case) can split off any elements of the application that are not intrinsically necessary to the main stated function of the development being applied for. This could mean that the housing and the Benidorms for instance could be removed and the golf course(s) alone may be approved. This would be better than what is currently applied for but would still require to be 'slid' south to remove it from the SSSI. There is no way to prejudge the outcome of the inquiry and I would not presume to do so or tell the reporters what they should do. I am quite certain that there are many people already trying to do just that.

So now we wait and see what the outcome and the reaction will be. I personally believe that if the outcome is as above, then the Trump Organisation will walk away, selling the property to another developer who will try again to push through something similar. That would be a missed opportunity for both this area and the Trump Organisation.

The Trump Organisation has a somewhat chequered reputation for environmental concerns with a couple of small awards in their belt and a lot of previous condemnation they have not left a 'green image' behind them. This may be the perfect opportunity for them to change that.

What do I mean? Well, if the original application is refused, instead of walking away in horror they could view this as the massive opportunity it is. Instead of building almost one thousand five hundred soulless accommodation units and a brash hotel, they could use the existing Menie House as a 'top end' base for eco tourists, perhaps with the assistance of the Aberdeen and North East Scotland Family History Society they could offer a bespoke service with the assistance of local bus companies and taxi firms they could do a 'family roots' type operation.

When the hotel is built, and one probably would be built, keep it in style with the local vernacular, but make it sustainable with solar panels and micro generation for power along with rainwater harvesting and similar systems. These are all possible and not that much more expensive than conventional building techniques, especially when done in volume. It would probably help their case if they were to make sure that all food served at the development is organic and free from GM contamination as well as being locally sourced.

There is enough land here that a coppicing programme could be initiated for firewood or other fuels, assuming that salt tolerant species are chosen; unlike those shown on the drawings for the golf course that would possibly not survive in the climate here.

They could still build some houses, but make them eco friendly. Design the housing to be earth sheltered dwellings with ground source heat pumps and other sustainable forms of heating and building control, possibly even zero emission with passive heating requirements. All are simple and easy to do with just a little effort and forethought. It is quite possible that this could become a centre of excellence for 'green' building and research, bearing in mind the ready supply of engineers and organisations working in these fields already based in Aberdeen, or if not working in these fields yet, willing to work in these fields. It is a perfect opportunity for the Trump Organisation to change their image in the eyes of the world and go from being a brash property developer with a possibly less than perfect environmental record to being a campaigner for a better future for all on this planet.

With recognition of Trump family history and the stated aims for wanting to build here in the first place it could be even be called 'The Mary Anne MacLeod Environmental Research Centre'.

14. References and further information

The two websites that have been generally against the development for the duration of the campaign are here.

www.menielinks.com

www.meniescotland.co.uk

The Trump Organisations own website which describes the development from their point of view is here

www.trumpgolfscotland.com

Aberdeenshire Council have their own website and you can access the earlier details and the drawings etc as submitted via the planning link on the right hand side of the page using the reference APP/2006/4605

www.aberdeenshire.gov.uk

The Scottish Wildlife Trust also have their own website with a campaign running as well, it can be accessed at

www.swt.org.uk

The Scottish Parliament website is here.

www.scottish.parliament.uk

Lightning Source UK Ltd.
Milton Keynes UK
UKOW032005070613

211938UK00001B/4/P